SCHOLASTIC

New York · Toronto · London · Auckland · Sydney
Mexico City · New Delhi · Hong Kong · Buenos Aires

Teaching *Resources*

Edited by Immacula A. Rhodes

Cover design by Scott Davis

Interior design by Sydney Wright

Illustrations by Teresa Anderko, Maxie Chambliss,
Kate Flanagan, Rusty Fletcher, and Sydney Wright

ISBN: 978-0-545-54135-0
Text and illustrations © 2013 by Scholastic Inc.
All rights reserved. Published by Scholastic Inc.
Printed in the U.S.A..

2 3 4 5 6 7 8 9 10   40   20 19 18 17 16 15 14

Contents

Introduction

Phonics Trees offers an engaging and fun way for kids to master essential phonics skills and concepts. Research shows that a strong foundation in phonics is an important component in building reading confidence and fluency. In his book *Phonics From A to Z* (Scholastic, 2006, revised), reading specialist Wiley Blevins notes that the faster children can decode words, the more words they recognize by sight, the more time and energy they have to devote to the meaning of the text (Freedman and Calfee, 1984; LaBerge and Samuels, 1974). Blevins cites Cunningham's (1995) observation that the brain works as a "pattern detector." Since blends, digraphs, and many vowel sounds contain reliable sound-spelling patterns, learning to recognize these common patterns helps children more easily and automatically decode new or unfamiliar words. This "automaticity" helps lay the foundation for long-term reading success.

The activities in this book give children lots of practice in decoding words using their knowledge of phonics. And writing the missing letters to complete the words provides even more opportunities for children to develop phonemic awareness skills and also helps boost spelling skills.

You can use the phonics trees with the whole class or in small groups. Or place them in a learning center for children to use independently or in pairs. The activities are ideal for children of all learning styles, ELL students, and for RTI instruction. And best of all, the phonics trees take only a few minutes to complete, making them a quick way to integrate phonics instruction into the school day.

How to Use the Phonics Trees

Completing a phonics tree is easy and fun. To begin, distribute copies of the activity page for the phonics skill you want to teach. Point out the phonics concept on the basket that's under the tree and name it. Then have children do the following:

Check pages 6–8 for a list of words that can be created for each phonics tree.

1 Look at the letter and letter combinations on the tree trunk. Sound out the letter(s) in front of each word stem on the apples to see if it makes an actual word.

2 If the letter(s) makes a word, write it on that apple to spell out the word. (Note that some letters might work with more than one word stem.) Point out that the word on the last apple will name the item to the right of the tree.

3 Use a different letter or letter combination with each word stem. After filling in all the apples, read the words aloud, pointing to each word while saying it.

Activities to Extend Learning

Use these activities to give children additional opportunities to practice phonics skills.

Make Your Own Tree: Use the template on page 64 to create your own phonics trees. To prepare, write the phonics skill of your choice on the basket. Label each apple with a different word that contains the target skill, using a blank line for the first letter(s) of the word. List the missing letter or letters from the apples on the tree trunk. Then copy a class supply of the page, distribute to children, and have them complete the activity. You might also give copies of the template to children so they can make their own phonics trees.

Phonics Apples: Write words that contain the phonics skill of your choice on red apple cutouts (one word per apple). Put the apples in a learning center. Then have student pairs use the apples as flash cards. One child can hold up one card at a time as the other child reads the word on it. To extend, have children work together to put the words in alphabetical order.

Phonics Shape Books: For shape books, mask the apples on a copy of the tree template (page 64) and make colored copies of the tree on sturdy paper. Also, cut a class supply of plain paper into quarters. To make a book, have children cut out the tree, then stack and staple 6–8 pages to the treetop. Ask them to choose a phonics concept (or assign phonics skills to children) and write it on the trunk. Then have children write one word that contains their phonics skill on each page, illustrating those words, if desired. Invite children to read their completed shape books with partners.

Phonics Memory: To make game cards for this familiar game, choose a phonics concept, such as long vowels or consonant blends. Label 20–24 red apple cutouts with different words that exemplify each concept, creating two apples for each specific skill. For example, for consonant blends, you might label the apples with *brand* and *bride*, *slip* and *slug*, *train* and *truck*, and so on. Then invite children to use the cards to play Memory. Each time they find the two apples with words containing the same phonics skill, they keep the match.

Musical Word Walk: Label sheets of paper with words that exemplify several different phonics skills, checking that each word belongs to a pair. Arrange the pages word-side down in a looped path. Then have children walk along the outside of the path while music plays. Periodically stop the music, have children pick up the nearest sheet, and then find another child with a word that contains the same phonics concept.

Connections to the Common Core State Standards

The Common Core State Standards Initiative (CCSSI) has outlined learning expectations in English Language Arts for students at different grade levels. The activities in this book align with the following Foundational Skills for Reading for students in grades K–2. For more information, visit the CCSSI Web site at www.corestandards.org.

Print Concepts
RF.K.1, RF.1.1. Demonstrate understanding of the organization and basic features of print.
RF.K.1a

Phonological Awareness
RF.K.2, RF.1.2. Demonstrate understanding of spoken words, syllables, and sounds (phonemes).
RF.K.2b, RF.K.2c, RF.K.2d, RF.K.2e
RF.1.2a, R.1.2b, R.1.2c, R.1.2d

Phonics and Word Recognition
RF.K.3, RF.1.3, RF.2.3. Know and apply grade-level phonics and word analysis skills in decoding words.
RF.K.3a, RF.K.3b, RF.K.3c, RF.K.3d
RF.1.3a, RF.1.3b, RF.1.3c
RF.2.3a, RF.2.3b

Fluency
RF.K.4. Read emergent-reader texts with purpose and understanding.
RF.1.4, RF.2.4. Read with sufficient accuracy and fluency to support comprehension.
RF.1.4a, RF.1.4c
RF.2.4a, RF.2.4c

Phonics Word Lists

This handy list includes the words that can be made with the letters and word stems on each activity page. Each word in bold print names the item to the right of the tree and should appear on the last apple on that tree.

Short a *(page 9)*
cab, crab, dab, flab, jab, lab, stab

back, crack, flack, hack, jack, lack, pack, rack, snack, stack, track

bag, crag, flag, hag, lag, rag, snag, stag

cram, dam, gram, jam, ram, yam, tram

camp, cramp, damp, lamp, ramp, stamp, tramp

bank, crank, dank, flank, lank, rank, stank, yank

cap, flap, lap, map, rap, snap, trap, yap

has

bat, **cat**, hat, pat, rat, flat

bath, math, path

Short a *(page 10)*
cab, dab, gab, grab, lab, nab, slab

back, clack, hack, lack, pack, sack, slack

bad, clad, dad, glad, grad, had, lad, mad, pad, sad

bag, gag, hag, lag, nag, sag, wag

clam, dam, ham, slam

camp, clamp, damp, lamp

ban, can, clan, **man**, pan, than

band, grand, hand, land, sand

bat, cat, hat, mat, pat, sat, slat, that

batch, catch, hatch, latch, match, patch

Short e *(page 11)*
bed, fed, led, red, wed, shed

deft, heft, left

beg, leg

bell, dell, fell, shell, smell, tell, well, yell

den, hen, ten, when

bent, dent, lent, rent, tent, went

desk

dress, less

best, jest, lest, **nest**, rest, test, west

bet, get, jet, let, net, wet, yet

Short e *(page 12)*
web

check, deck, heck, neck, peck

bed, led, red, sled, wed

help

den, hen, men, pen, ten, then

bend, lend, mend, rend, send, tend, trend

bent, dent, lent, rent, sent, tent, went

chess, less, mess, tress

best, chest, jest, lest, nest, pest, rest, test, west

bet, jet, let, met, net, pet, set, wet

Short i *(page 13)*
brick, flick, hick, kick, lick, nick, pick, sick, thick, tick

bid, hid, kid, lid

gift, lift, shift, sift

big, brig, fig, gig, **pig**

milk, silk

bill, fill, gill, hill, kill, mill, pill, sill, till

bin, fin, kin, pin, shin, thin, tin

brink, fink, kink, link, mink, pink, sink, think

flip, hip, lip, nip, ship, sip, tip

fix, mix, six

Short i *(page 14)*
crib, fib, rib

chick, hick, lick, pick, sick, tick, wick

big, dig, fig, gig, pig, rig, swig, wig

milk, silk

dim, him, rim, skim, swim, whim

bin, chin, fin, pin, skin, tin, win

chink, fink, link, mink, pink, rink, sink, wink

chip, dip, hip, lip, rip, sip, skip, tip, whip

dish, fish, wish, swish

fix, mix, six

Short o *(page 15)*
cob, fob, gob, job, lob, sob

cock, dock, frock, jock, lock, sock, stock, tock

cod, god, nod, pod, sod

bog, cog, dog, fog, frog, hog, jog, log

loft, soft

doll

chomp, pomp, stomp

chop, cop, hop, lop, pop, stop, top

cot, dot, got, hot, jot, lot, not, pot, tot

box, fox, lox, pox

Short o *(page 16)*
blob, fob, job, mob, rob, sob

block, clock, dock, jock, mock, rock, shock, sock, stock

clod, mod, nod, plod, pod, rod, sod

blog, bog, clog, **dog**, fog, hog, jog

mom

clomp, pomp, romp, stomp

blond, bond, pond

clop, hop, mop, plop, pop, shop, sop, stop, top

blot, clot, dot, hot, jot, not, plot, pot, rot, shot, tot

box, fox, pox

Short u *(page 17)*
cub, dub, hub, nub, pub, rub, stub, sub, tub

buck, **duck**, luck, muck, pluck, puck, stuck, suck, tuck

bug, dug, hug, lug, mug, plug, pug, rug, tug

bum, gum, hum, mum, plum, rum, sum

bump, dump, hump, lump, plump, pump, rump, stump

bun, gun, nun, pun, run, stun, sun

crush, gush, hush, lush, mush, plush, rush

bust, crust, dust, gust, lust, must, rust

but, cut, gut, hut, nut, rut

buzz

Short u *(page 18)*
dub, grub, hub, pub, rub, sub

bug, dug, hug, jug, mug, plug, pug, rug

bum, gum, hum, mum, plum, rum, sum

bump, dump, grump, hump, jump, plump, pump, rump, trump

brunt, bunt, grunt, hunt,

bunk, dunk, funk, hunk, junk, plunk, punk, sunk, trunk

brunt, bunt, grunt, hunt, punt, runt

pup

bus, plus, pus

brush, gush, hush, mush, plush, rush

bust, dust, gust, just, must, rust, trust

Short o *(page 16)* — *a_e* *(page 19)*

a_e *(page 19)*

face, grace, lace, mace, pace, place, trace

fade, grade, made, trade, wade

cake, fake, lake, make, sake, **snake**, take, wake

dale, gale, male, pale, sale, tale, whale

came, dame, fame, game, lame, name, same, tame

cane, lane, mane, pane, plane, sane, wane

cape, gape, grape, nape, tape

date, fate, gate, grate, late, mate, plate

cave, gave, grave, pave, save, wave

daze, faze, gaze, graze, laze, maze

a_e *(page 20)*
brace, mace, pace, race

jade, made, shade, wade

page, rage, sage, wage

bake, brake, flake, make, rake, sake, shake, take, wake

bale, hale, kale, male, pale, sale, shale, tale, vale, wale

flame, same, shame, tame

base, vase

baste, haste, paste, taste, waste

hate, mate, rate, **skate**

brave, pave, rave, save, shave, wave

i_e *(page 21)*
lice, **mice**, rice, vice

bide, chide, hide, ride, stride, tide, wide

fife, life, rife, strife, wife

bike, hike, like, pike, strike

bile, file, mile, pile, rile, tile, vile, while

chime, lime, mime, time

fine, line, mine, pine, vine, whine

pipe, ripe, stripe, wipe

kite, mite, rite, white

chive, drive, five, hive, live, strive

i_e *(page 22)*
bride, pride, ride, side, slide, wide
fife, life, rife, wife
dike, like, pike
file, mile, pile, rile
dime, lime, mime, prime, slime
brine, dine, fine, line, mine,
    nine, pine, shine, wine
pipe, ripe, wipe
rise, wise
kite, mite, rite, site
dive, five, jive, live

o_e *(page 23)*
globe, lobe, robe
bode, code, node, rode
broke, coke, joke, stoke, woke
dole, hole, mole, role, stole,
    vole, whole
bone, cone, hone, lone, stone
cope, dope, hope, mope, nope,
    rope
hose, nose, rose, those
dote, note, rote, vote
cove, dove, rove, stove, wove
doze

o_e *(page 24)*
lobe, probe, robe
coke, poke, smoke
hole, mole, pole, role, sole, vole
home, tome
clone, cone, drone, hone,
    lone, prone, tone, zone
cope, hope, mope, nope,
    pope, rope
close, **hose**, nose, pose,
    prose, rose
note, rote, tote, vote
clove, cove, drove, rove
froze

ai *(page 25)*
braid, paid
bail, fail, hail, jail, nail, pail,
    sail, **snail**, wail
brain, chain, pain
faint, paint, saint
braise, chaise, praise
waist
bait, wait

ai *(page 26)*
maid, paid, raid, staid
fail, mail, nail, pail, quail, rail,
    trail, wail
claim, maim
drain, gain, main, pain, rain,
    stain, **train**
faint, paint, quaint
raise
gait, trait, wait

ay *(page 27)*
bay, clay, hay, **jay**, may, play,
    say, spray, tray, way

ai, ay *(page 28)*
laid, maid, paid, raid, staid
fail, grail, **mail**, nail, pail,
    rail, wail
gain, grain, main, pain, rain,
    stain, strain, vain
faint, paint
wait
day, gay, gray, lay, may, nay,
    pay, ray, stay, stray, way

ea *(page 29)*
bead, lead, plead, read
leaf
beak, leak, peak, sneak
deal, heal, meal, peal, real,
    seal, teal, veal
beam, ream, seam, team
bean, clean, lean, mean
cheap, heap, leap, reap
lease, please, tease
beast, feast, least
beat, cheat, cleat, feat, heat,
    meat, peat, pleat, seat, treat

ea *(page 30)*
flea, sea
beach, bleach, reach
bead, **read**
bleak, creak, speak, weak
deal, heal, meal, real, seal
beam, cream, ream, seam
bean, dean, mean, wean
heap, reap
beat, bleat, feat, heat, meat,
    neat, seat, wheat
heave, leave, weave

ee *(page 31)*
bee, fee, flee, see, tee, tree,
    wee
beech, speech
deed, feed, heed, need, reed,
    seed, speed, weed
beef, reef
cheek, peek, reek, seek, week
feel, heel, keel, peel, reel
keen, seen, sheen, teen
beep, cheep, keep, peep,
    sheep, weep
beet, feet, fleet, sheet
teeth

ee *(page 32)*
bee, free, lee, see, tee, whee
deed, freed, greed, reed,
    seed, speed
beef, reef
cheek, leek, meek, peek, reek,
    seek, sleek
keel, peel, reel, wheel
deem, seem, teem
beep, cheep, deep, jeep,
    keep, peep, seep, sleep
cheese
beet, greet, meet, sleet
freeze, wheeze

ea, ee *(page 33)*
beach, peach, reach, teach
beak, creak, leak, peak, sneak,
    weak
deal, heal, meal, peal, real,
    seal, steal, teal
beam, cream, dream, ream,
    seam, steam, team
bean, dean, lean, mean, wean
creed, deed, feed, heed, reed,
    seed, steed, weed
feel, heel, peel, reel, steel
queen, seen, teen
beep, deep, creep, peep, seep,
    steep, weep
beet, feet, meet

i, y *(page 34)*
child, mild, wild
climb
bind, find, hind, kind, mind,
    rind, wind
by, cry, my, sky, why

ie, igh *(page 35)*
die, lie, **pie**, tie
high, nigh, sigh, thigh
bright, fight, flight, light, night,
    sight, slight, tight

oa *(page 36)*
whoa
coach, poach, roach
goad, load, road, toad
loaf
coal, foal, goal
foam, roam
groan, loan, moan
soap
boast, coast, roast, toast
boat, coat, **goat**

ow *(page 37)*
bow, **crow**, grow, low, mow,
    row, show, snow, stow,
    throw, tow
bowl
grown, shown, thrown

o, oe *(page 38)*
go, no, so
doe, foe, hoe, roe, toe, woe
bold, cold, fold, gold, hold,
    mold, sold, told
roll

ou *(page 39)*
couch, grouch, pouch
cloud
foul
bounce, pounce, trounce
bound, found, ground, hound,
    mound, pound, round,
    sound
house, grouse, **mouse**, rouse
bout, clout, grout, pout, rout,
    shout, trout
mouth, south

ou *(page 40)*
loud
noun
flounce, jounce, pounce
hound, mound, pound
count, mount
blouse, house, louse, mouse
lout, pout, **scout**, snout
mouth

ow *(page 41)*
chow, cow, how, now, pow,
    prow
crowd
chowder, powder
dowel, towel, trowel
cower, power, tower
cowl, fowl, howl, prowl
clown, crown, down, town

ow *(page 42)*
bow, brow, **cow**, pow, vow
crowd
powder
bowel, dowel, towel, vowel
bower, cower, flower, power,
    tower
cowl, growl
brown, crown, down, frown,
    gown, town

(continued)

ou, ow *(page 43)*
cloud, loud
bounce, flounce, pounce
bound, found, hound, mound, pound, sound
house, louse, mouse
bout, clout, flout, pout, shout, **sprout**, tout
bow, chow, cow, how, now, pow, sow
chowder, powder
bower, cower, flower, power, shower, tower
cowl, fowl, howl
clown, frown, town

oi, oy *(page 44)*
choice, voice
boil, coil, foil
coin, join
joint, point
noise
poison
foist, joist, moist
boy, coy, joy
voyage
loyal

ar *(page 45)*
bar, car, char, far, **jar**, mar, par, scar, star, tar
march, parch, starch
card, hard, lard, shard, yard
scarf
barge, charge, large
bark, dark, hark, lark, park, shark, stark
charm, farm, harm
barn, darn, yarn
carp, harp, sharp, tarp
cart, chart, dart, mart, part, smart, start, tart

ar *(page 46)*
car, char, jar, mar, par, spar, star
march, parch, starch
card, hard, lard
garden, harden
charge, large
dark, hark, lark, mark, park, spark, stark
charm, harm
darn, **yarn**
cart, chart, dart, mart, part, start
party

air *(page 47)*
chair, fair, flair, hair, lair, pair, stair

are *(page 48)*
bare, blare, care, dare, flare, hare, pare, rare, scare, share, **square**, stare, ware

ir, ur *(page 49)*
fir, sir, stir
bird, gird, third
girl, swirl, twirl
first, thirst
shirt, skirt
surf, turf
curl, furl, hurl
burn, turn
curse, nurse, purse
curt, hurt

or *(page 50)*
for, nor
porch, scorch, torch
cord
forge, gorge
cork, fork, pork, stork
dorm, form, norm, storm
born, corn, horn, morn, scorn, shorn, torn, thorn
horse
fort, port, short, sort, tort
forth, north

au *(page 51)*
sauce
caught, taught
haul, maul
fault, vault
haunch, launch, paunch, staunch
laundry
cause, clause, pause

au, aw *(page 52)*
sauce
caught, taught
cause, clause, pause
caw, claw, draw, **paw**, raw, saw, straw
hawk
bawl, crawl, drawl
drawn, pawn, sawn, yawn

al, aw *(page 53)*
balk, chalk, stalk, talk
ball, hall, pall, small, squall, stall, tall
halt, salt
law, paw, saw, squaw
hawk, squawk
dawn, lawn, pawn, sawn, yawn
lawyer

ew, ue *(page 54)*
blew, chew, dew, few, flew, mew, new, pew, stew, threw
newt
blue, cue, due, glue, hue, sue, true

oo *(moon)* *(page 55)*
boo, coo, goo, moo, too, zoo
brood, food, mood
goof, proof, roof
cool, drool, fool, stool
boom, broom, loom, room, zoom
boon, goon, loon, moon, soon, swoon
coop, droop, loop, scoop, swoop
goose, loose, moose
boot, loot, root, scoot, toot
booth, smooth, tooth

oo *(book)* *(page 56)*
good, hood, stood, wood
hoof, woof
book, brook, **cook**, hook, look, shook, took
cookie
wool
foot

l-blends *(page 57)*
place
clad, glad
claim
slice
blind
flower, glower, slower

r-blends *(page 58)*
dragon
price
friend
grin
broke
crowd
true

l-blends, r-blends
(page 59)
glance
crane, plane
blast
bream, cream, dream, gleam
green
sleeve
flesh, fresh
bride, glide, slide
bloat, float, gloat
closet

s-blends *(page 60)*
stand, strand
scrap, slap, snap, strap, swap
scarf
spread, stead
screech, speech
sleet, street, sweet
squirm
slob, snob
smooth
skunk, spunk, stunk

r-blends, s-blends
(page 61)
grape
scare, snare, spare, square, stare
start
spend
brick, prick, stick
gripe, snipe, stripe
prize
frog
brown, crown, frown, grown
snug

l-blends, digraphs
(page 62)
shale, whale
plane
sharp
bleach
thread
them
chicken
chide, glide, slide
clone, phone, shone, throne
chute, flute

s-blends, digraphs
(page 63)
charm, swarm
snatch, swatch, thatch
spree, thee, three, whee
cheese
step
there, where
chick, slick, stick, thick
phone, stone, shone, throne
should
shout, snout, sprout, stout

Name: _____ Date: _____

___as

___ap

___amp

___ath

___ank

___ab

___ack

___am

___ag

___at

j	h	m	fl
b	p	r	st
tr	l	cr	c
d	sn	y	gr

Short a

___ack

___at

___am

___amp

___ag

___atch

___ab

___and

___ad

___an

s	b	l	h
w	sl	d	n
cl	p	sk	c
gr	m	g	th

Short a

Name: _____ Date: _____

___esk

___ent

___eg

___en

___ed

___ell

___eft

___et

___ess

___est

w	b	f	t
y	sm	j	dr
h	d	sh	n
wh	r	l	g

Short e

Name: _____ Date: _____

___et

___elp

___en

___est

___ed

___eck

___ess

___ent

___end

___eb

n	tr	p	ch
r	t	l	d
th	w	h	m
j	s	b	sl

Short e

Name: _____ Date: _____

____ilk

____ix

____ill

____ink

____ift

____id

____in

____ip

____ick

____ig

v	sh	t	f
l	n	k	m
th	p	fl	h
g	s	b	br

Short i

Name: _____ Date: _____

___ish

___ig

___ix

___im

___ilk

___ink

___ib

___ip

___in

___ick

sk	l	d	sw
s	ch	cr	f
g	m	wh	t
w	p	r	h

Short i

___og

___omp

___od

___ox

___ock

___op

___oft

___ob

___ot

___oll

s	l	g	st
h	ch	d	c
j	b	fr	t
th	p	n	f

Short o

Name: _____ Date: _____

___om

___ox

___op

___ob

___ock

___od

___omp

___ot

___ond

___og

s	pl	t	bl
st	j	p	cl
m	d	f	r
n	h	sh	b

Short o

Phonics Trees © 2013 by Scholastic Teaching Resources, page 16

Name: _____ Date: _____

___uzz

___un

___ump

___ug

___ut

___ush

___ub

___um

___ust

___uck

pl	l	cr	p
b	st	h	wh
r	c	s	m
g	t	d	n

Short u

___up

___unk

___um

___unt

___ush

___us

___ust

___ub

___ump

___ug

gr	s	f	br
d	tr	pl	p
j	b	g	k
r	v	h	m

Short u

Name: _____ Date: _____

___ame

___ace

___ave

___ate

___ale

___ane

___ape

___ade

___aze

___ake

s	w	wh	m
c	tr	g	d
t	n	p	pl
gr	f	sn	l

a_e

Name: _____ Date: _____

___ale

___ave

___age

___ade

___ace

___aste

___ase

___ame

___ake

___ate

m	s	br	sk
sh	w	j	v
k	pr	t	b
r	h	p	fl

a_e

Name: _____ Date: _____

___ile

___ide

___ive

___ike

___ite

___ime

___ife

___ine

___ipe

___ice

k	p	v	m
str	r	l	h
w	ch	t	dr
g	b	f	wh

i_e

Phonics Trees © 2013 by Scholastic Teaching Resources, page 21

Name: _____ Date: _____

___ike

___ime

___ipe

___ile

___ife

___ine

___ide

___ive

___ise

___ite

n k f c

l sh j m

pr r sl w

s d p br

i_e

Phonics Trees © 2013 by Scholastic Teaching Resources, page 22

___oze

___ove

___obe

___oke

___ole

___ote

___ode

___ose

___ope

___one

v	n	th	j
c	st	d	br
m	b	h	r
gl	l	wh	w

o_e

Name: _____ Date: _____

___ope

___ove

___ome

___ole

___oze

___obe

___ote

___oke

___one

___ose

z   fr   l   pr

cl   v   sm   c

p   h   n   s

r   t   dr   m

o_e

___aist

___aise

___ait

___ain

___aint

___aid

___ail

s   n   p   b

br   f   sn   h

w   pr   j   ch

ai

Name: _____ Date: _____

___aise

___aid

___aim

___ait

___ail

___aint

___ain

w	tr	n	st
m	f	cl	g
dr	r	p	qu

ai

Name: _____   Date: _____

_____ay   _____ay   _____ay

_____ay   _____ay   _____ay   _____ay

_____ay   _____ay   _____ay

m   x   pl   z
k   b   j   h
cl   c   w   spr
t   tr   s   f

ay

Phonics Trees © 2013 by Scholastic Teaching Resources, page 27

___ait

___ay

___aint

___ay

___aid

___ay

___ay

___ain

___ay

___ail

gr	y	n	str
v	l	st	r
w	m	d	g
f	th	p	bl

ai
ay

Name: _____ Date: _____

___eaf

___eap

___ead

___ease

___east

___eat

___ean

___eam

___eal

___eak

r	l	d	t
m	pl	v	ch
cl	f	sn	s
p	tr	b	h

ea

Phonics Trees © 2013 by Scholastic Teaching Resources, page 29

___eap

___ea

___eave

___ean

___eal

___each

___eak

___eam

___eat

___ead

k	f	r	fl
w	sp	h	n
s	d	wh	cr
bl	b	g	m

ea

Name: _____ Date: _____

___eeth

___ee

___eef

___eed

___eet

___een

___eech

___eek

___eel

___eep

sp	k	tr	r
d	t	n	fl
w	f	h	b
p	ch	sh	s

ee

Name: _____   Date: _____

___eese

___eef

___eep

___eek

___eel

___eeze

___eem

___eet

___eed

___ee

sp	p	fr	d
k	wh	j	gr
s	l	r	t
b	m	sl	ch

ee

Phonics Trees © 2013 by Scholastic Teaching Resources, page 32

Name: _____ Date: _____

___each

___eet

___eak

___eam

___ean

___eep

___eel

___eed

___eal

___een

b	p	s	l
qu	w	cr	m
f	dr	d	h
st	t	sn	r

ea
ee

___y

___ind

___y

___ind

___y

___ild

___y

___imb

___y

___ild

t	j	ch	sk
cr	s	w	m
f	b	k	h
p	wh	r	cl

i
y

___igh

___ie

___ight

___ie

___ight

___ight

___igh

___ie

l   n   fl   s

d   sl   t   f

br   h   p   th

ie
igh

Name: _____   Date: _____

___oaf

___oach

___oam

___oal

___oap

___oad

___oa

___oast

___oan

___oat

c	g	gr	l
wh	b	p	d
r	st	f	n
s	m	t	sn

oa

Name: _____   Date: _____

___own

___ow

___ow

___ow

___ow

___owl

___ow

___ow

___ow

___ow

h	thr	l	d
st	v	sn	m
f	cr	b	g
gr	r	t	sh

ow

___oll

___old

___oe

___o

___oe

___oe

___old

___old

___o

___oe

r	w	h	m
f	sh	s	d
t	c	cl	n
fr	b	g	sm

o
oe

Name: _____ Date: _____

___oul

___out

___ounce

___oud

___ound

___outh

___ouch

___ouse

r   h   s   sh

cl   tr   b   c

p   m   gr   f

ou

___outh

___oud

___oun

___ount

___ounce

___ouse

___ound

___out

n   d   sc   m

h   sn   j   l

bl   p   c   fl

ou

Name: _____ Date: _____

___owd

___owl

___owder

___owel

___ower

___ow

___own

tr   cl   d   p

c   n   cr   t

pr   f   h   ch

ow

___owel

___owd

___ower

___own

___owl

___owder

___ow

v   cr   gr   d

br   fl   b   g

p   fr   c   t

ow

Name: _____   Date: _____

___ow

___ower

___ouse

___owder

___ound

___own

___oud

___ounce

___owl

___out

t	fr	sh	b
ch	s	p	cl
m	fl	l	f
c	n	spr	h

ou
ow

___oise

___oin

___oist

___oison

___oint

___oyage

___oil

___oyal

___oice

___oy

tr	b	g	cl
p	wh	d	v
n	j	l	fr
ch	f	m	c

oi
oy

Name: _____   Date: _____

___ark

___art

___arp

___arch

___arge

___arn

___arf

___ard

___arm

___ar

t	j	st	m
b	sm	h	c
sh	d	ch	p
y	f	l	sc

ar

Name: _____ Date: _____

___arty

___art

___arm

___ar

___arch

___ark

___arden

___ard

___arge

___arn

d	sp	g	l
s	z	ch	c
bl	m	h	st
j	r	y	p

ar

____air

____air

____air

____air

____air

____air

____air

s   v   f   k

l   fl   st   g

h   p   j   ch

air

Name: _____ Date: _____

___are

___are

___are

___are

___are

___are

___are

___are

___are

___are

fl   b   r   st
w   p   sc   c
z   sh   j   h
bl   d   n   squ

are

Phonics Trees © 2013 by Scholastic Teaching Resources, page 48

Name: _____ Date: _____

___urt

___urn

___irt

___urse

___url

___ird

___ir

___urf

___irst

___irl

sw	n	s	tw
h	sh	j	f
th	t	sk	c
g	b	p	st

ir, ur

Phonics Trees © 2013 by Scholastic Teaching Resources, page 49

Name: _____ Date: _____

____or

____ord

____orth

____orge

____ork

____orch

____orm

____orn

____ort

____orse

st   t   g   m

y   b   sh   d

c   f   p   th

s   sc   h   n

or

Name: _____   Date: _____

___auce

___aught

___aunch

___ault

___ause

___aul

___aundry

th l st f

p c h s

m t v cl

au

Name: _____ Date: _____

___awk

___auce

___aught

___awl

___ause

___awn

___aw

h str y c

s t dr r

cl b p cr

au
aw

Name: _____ Date: _____

___awyer

___awk

___awn

___alk

___aw

___alt

___all

l   st   b   p

t   h   sm   d

ch   s   y   squ

al
aw

Name: _____ Date: _____

___ue

___ew

___ue

___ue

___ew

___ue

___ew

___ew

___ue

___ewt

w	f	tr	n
bl	c	d	gl
s	thr	m	p
fl	h	ch	st

ew
ue

___oof

___oon

___oo

___oop

___ooth

___oot

___ool

___oom

___ood

___oose

t	sm	r	sw
br	z	pr	l
s	c	f	g
dr	m	sc	b

oo

____ool

____oof

____oot

____ood

____ookie

____ook

st b c g

h s sh t

w l f br

oo

____ace

____ice

____ind

____aim

____ad

____ower

bl   shr   cr   squ

st   pl   gl   ch

cl   fl   sl   th

l-blends

Name: _____ Date: _____

____ice

____ue

____in

____iend

____oke

____owd

____agon

br   q   w   pr

f   cr   fr   squ

tr   z   gr   dr

r-blends

Name: _____   Date: _____

___ance

___eeve

___ast

___ane

___oset

___een

___oat

___eam

___esh

___ide

pl	x	j	fr
g	cr	cl	n
br	z	dr	gr
gl	bl	fl	sl

l-blends
r-blends

___eech

___and

___ead

___eet

___ap

___ooth

___arf

___ob

___irm

___unk

st	sp	w	sn
x	squ	str	k
scr	v	sw	sl
sk	sc	sm	spr

s-blends

Name: _____   Date: _____

___end

___ipe

___own

___are

___ug

___ize

___ick

___art

___ape

___og

sc	sp	gr	cr
q	sn	pr	str
fr	z	squ	v
br	sk	st	tw

r-blends
s-blends

Phonics Trees © 2013 by Scholastic Teaching Resources, page 61

Name: _____ Date: _____

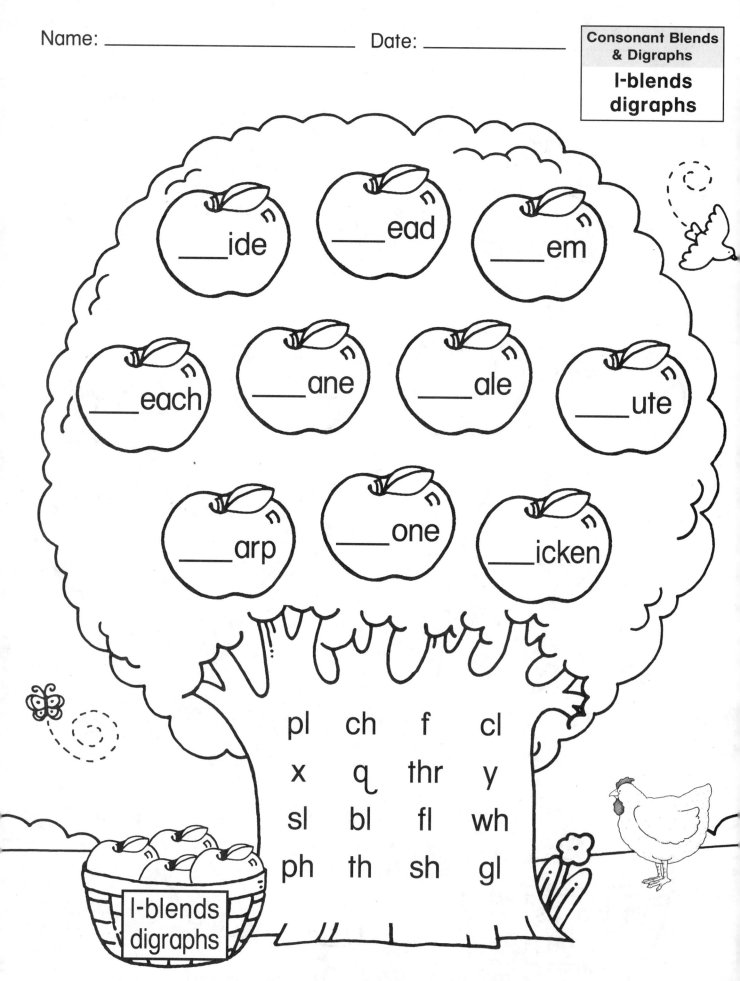

___ide

___ead

___em

___each

___ane

___ale

___ute

___arp

___one

___icken

pl	ch	f	cl
x	q	thr	y
sl	bl	fl	wh
ph	th	sh	gl

l-blends
digraphs

Name: _____   Date: _____

___ould

___atch

___ep

___ick

___ee

___arm

___ere

___one

___out

___eese

sh	thr	v	sm
wh	j	st	x
th	q	ch	sn
sw	spr	ph	sl

s-blends
digraphs

Name: _____ Date: _____